Lessons I Learned From the Fire—A Cautionary Tale

Lessons I Learned From the Fire—A Cautionary Tale

Tonya D Floyd

CONTENTS

First Printing, 2025

1

Introduction

Introduction

Ecclesiastes 9:11 says, '... the swift do not always win the race, nor do the mighty win the battle, nor do the wise always have the food, nor do the intelligent always have the riches, nor do those with knowledge always have success ....' Ain't that the truth?! Sometimes we lose; sometimes we lose big. And sometimes it costs us a pretty penny, among other things. I got so mad about this the other day, I thought I was having a stroke. My eyes started twitching and my head was pounding. I could hear the blood rushing through my head.

It seems like every time I turn around, somebody is trying to take/steal something from me. I've been stewing over this one particular injustice I've suffered for a while now, thinking about the best way to share it—making sure my motivation was pure enough, wondering if the delivery would hit its target, deciding whether anyone would even care about it or not. You know how it goes. What does my suffering have to do with anyone else out there? I pray it helps somebody though. I really do.

Well, I concluded that I have the right to share my experience, but I also feel an obligation to educate others about the potential dangers of not knowing the process, hiring the wrong company, and what it may eventually cost you. I've done my research (I know; I'm late), and I know I'm not alone. Many others have been burned in one way or another by this particular entity, going back at least 25 years.

I wasn't shocked per se, but I was astounded and disappointed by the number of times I found the name listed in complaints. Now, I know somebody out there is thinking I should've done my research before hiring them, or at the very least I should've cut ties with them before it got too deep. Funny enough, that's the first lesson I learned, and it's exactly the advice I'm giving you right now.

Lesson 1: Learn from my enormous mistake and do your research on any company BEFORE you sign on the dotted line for anything, ever. Search them up in multiple databases. Read reviews. Consider their years in business. Get a feel for the players/owners/representatives in person to see if any red flags pop up during the interaction. Do not ignore those if they do pop up.

Trust your instincts. Ask pointed questions. That said, some folks are slicker than grease, and really good at selling snake oil. Don't blame yourself if they get over on you; you're just a decent person who needed a service performed, and you fell into a trap you never saw coming, because you expect professionals to have integrity. They've probably been doing this for a while though. If you catch it in time, there may be legal recourse or consumer protections available to you.

It's no excuse, and I know better now, but I was operating on trust when I chose to do business with this entity. I was completely out of my element, they came to me as a referral, and I was a decent, honest, hard-working homeowner who had just experienced a traumatic event. I wanted to get back into my home as soon as possible, and I trusted the professionals I hired to do a job they appeared to be more than capable of doing. It never occurred to me what was about to happen.

Lesson 2: Be prepared; anything can happen. Walk around your home and take random pics of things, generally noting where things are and capturing what you own. If you collect receipts like me, that helps too. If you ever have a disaster, fire, etc, you'll need to file a claim for your personal belongings, in great detail. The description will likely need to include each item's age, price, brand.

Familiarize yourself with your homeowner's insurance policy. General sections of coverage are Dwelling, Other Structures, Loss of Use, Personal Property, and you may have additional coverages. I'm not sure how it looks for renters, but same advice. Know what your coverage limits are and what each section entails. Adjust your policy and coverages as necessary.

2

It was just a regular Thursday morning....

It was just a regular Thursday morning....

See, I was minding my business at home one Thursday morning, around 7:30am. It was just my youngest son, our dog, and me. My son was getting dressed for school. At the moment, he was in my shower—because he had a tendency to move slowly and I needed to keep him on track so he didn't miss the school bus. I heard a funny "poof" sound coming from his bedroom beneath me. When I went to investigate, I stopped at the doorway, in shock? Disbelief? Amazement? I don't know exactly what the feeling was, but I had to move quickly to put out the little fire emanating from his nightstand, which was situated next to his bed.

So many thoughts, so many feelings, but no time. I ran to the hall closet where we kept the fire extinguisher, grabbed it, pulled the pin, aimed it at the base of the flame, and squeezed it. Nothing. What?! I went to the kitchen looking for something. Water? No, it's electrical. I went back to look at the flame like it would tell me what to use. By now, the little flame that was dancing where the branded motorcycle lamp that made the cool engine sounds used to sit was a much wider, much taller flame, and I knew there was only one thing to do. I ran upstairs, where my son was standing in a towel by now, and I barked some orders at him: "Put on these clothes RIGHT NOW, grab your shoes and run down to the car!"

He probably had questions, but maybe it was the way I spoke that made him hold those and just do what I said. I was wearing a strapless sundress and flip-flops at the time, which would have to do. I grabbed my purse and my cell phone, started down the stairs behind my son, and I yelled at the dog to come on. But by the time we got to the stairs, gray smoke was billowing upwards to where we were, and it was really hard to see in front of us. Then the smoke alarm started screeching. It was so loud and jarring! I told my son to just go down the stairs to the garage. Surely we knew the landscape well enough to do it without sight; right?

I thought we could make it, but because of the black smoke now pouring out of his bedroom, I quickly realized the dining room door was our only option. I diverted him to the back door, still calling for the dog, who must have given up because all I heard was howls and whines blending in with the alarm. Meanwhile, I dialed 911 and was talking to the dispatcher, who kept telling me to get out of the house. She firmly repeated a few times, "DO NOT GO BACK IN FOR THE DOG MS FLOYD." I stood outside the back door calling his name, but I knew he couldn't hear me over all the alarms now sounding. He was terrified. I had never seen him cower at anything before that day.

But then the smoke was all black, and I couldn't see my hand in front of my face. I just backed completely out the door and stood on the porch, feeling all kinds of crazy because WTF JUST HAPPENED?! It was so fast, so sneaky, so obnoxious, so overbearing. Black smoke just poured out of my house in front of me. It was a brief few seconds later that I heard the fire engines entering the development from the street behind me. The dispatcher was still in my ear asking me if everyone was out. I told her everyone but the dog. She reminded me again not to go inside, but there was no chance I would at this point. My son was fiddling with the gate at the side of the house. We had it rigged so the escape artist dog wouldn't let himself out at will.

Eventually, I saw firefighters coming from both sides of the house, and some went in the way we came out. I ended my call with the dispatcher. It literally just occurred to me that they must have gone in that way and unlocked the front door, because it was surely locked up tight. Then I heard the sounds of breaking glass above me. I moved to the side of the house, but they were breaking windows there too, so I moved to the sidewalk out front. I was stuck on stupid.

There were emergency vehicles up the block, people on both sides of the street watching, and I remember thinking *this is way too much attention for me*. In my adrenaline-fueled state, I was still very embarrassed. Then I felt exposed, vulnerable, and wondered what would happen next. Clearly, I wasn't going back home like any other day.

My son had found a friend and begun a game of chase, like nothing was happening. I have the friend's mother to thank for that. A few neighbors came out to check on us, and this particular neighbor gave my son a uniform shirt to wear to school. Good idea; you go to school, and I'll deal with all of whatever this is. Not long after that, my dog came flying through the open gate, running in circles, coughing, frantic. I told one of the firefighters where to find his leash, so I could at least try to get him under control. I was able to stash him in another neighbor's yard two houses down. Naturally, he escaped though. The kids chased him around the neighborhood and finally brought him back. But at least they had something to focus on. At some point, it was safe to just stick him back in my own yard.

Though it probably seems like a chunk of time had gone by, we were still only a few short minutes out from when I originally found the flame. The smoke filled the house within two minutes, tops. The time between finding the flame and getting out of the house was maybe one minute. The fire house is two minutes from my house, so the firefighters arrived swiftly, and had the fire out maybe ten minutes after I called. All in all, I might have been outside for a solid fifteen minutes before I was told the fire was out and I could come see the damages.

Before I could do that, though, a friend called my cell. I remember telling him I would have to call him back because my house was just on fire. His response grabbed me: "I know. Is everybody all right?" Huh? I started looking around. *Where is this dude, and how does he know?* I said, "What do you mean you know? How?" He said, "It's a long story, but listen; a lot of people are gonna approach you and try to get you to sign stuff. Don't sign anything, and don't talk to any of them until I get there." Bet. Got it. Still stuck on stupid though.

He must have been on his way when he called, because I wasn't even done with my walk-through when he showed up. It felt reassuring to have him there, and seemingly on top of the situation, but

I still had questions. The fire chief came and talked to me; he gave me a card with information on how to get the fire report later.

Right after that, some men did approach me, asking about my representative, offering construction services, etc. My friend basically waved them off, but told them to leave their contact information. One guy approached, and they seemed familiar with each other. He told me to let this man's company board up my windows. So I agreed. After things calmed down a bit, which was maybe 30 minutes after I found the flame, he explained how he came to know about my situation and how he would help me navigate what came next.

Turns out my friend is a Public Adjuster; he and the other men got the same notification through some network that sends alerts about disasters in the area, like fire. I had never heard that term before, but he explained that Public Adjusters get paid to help you deal with insurance claims and navigate that whole process. I welcomed his expertise, and I signed a contract with him that same day.

I literally had no experience with any of these things. Within an hour, I had an emergency cash advance on the way from my insurance company, and I was to meet with a man from some company who would get me set up in temporary lodging. But before that, we took a slow walk through my property to assess the damage. Let me tell you it was a hot mess (it's funny now).

Water actively trickled down the stairs to the front door. Black powder lined the walls and gathered in the corners of the ceiling. Glass and other things lay broken on the floor, seemingly everywhere. I even had glass in some of my shoes. There were holes in random parts of the ceiling. Screens were removed from the windows, which were all opened—though some were not broken. The air smelled damp and yucky already. The power was cut immediately, so no lights or HVAC were running.

It looked like someone had run through the house and stomped on things, while throwing and kicking other things around. My son's room was soggy, and covered in blackness, the wall burnt to the studs in some places. White splashes were on the walls and ceiling. There were clothes and shoes piled on the bed—all soggy. My daughter's room next door was covered in black dust too. Carpet trashed. Downstairs, there was water EVERYWHERE. It still leaked through the ceiling fixtures, and some puddled on the table.

Every interior door throughout the house was opened. Upstairs, more black dust everywhere, and what looked like black silly string in some places. Lots of glass. All my bedroom windows were busted out. More ceiling stabs, and pink insulation hung down.

I made my way to the dresser and grabbed some smoky smelling jeans and a t-shirt before grabbing my work laptop and some important papers I kept in my closet. I got dressed, then I locked up and pulled the manual release to get my car from the garage. I retrieved my dog and thanked my neighbors for their support. Then I left my house just sitting there, ugly, violated, dirty, and feeling very much unlike home.

My next stop was the hotel where my Public Adjuster friend had arranged for us to meet the man who would secure our lodging. But I had to make a few phone calls along the way. I called my other kids, my parents, and my ex. I called some other people eventually. When I arrived at the extended stay hotel, the man introduced himself to me. He told me we would stay until he could find us a temporary house comparable in size/features to mine. He had me sign for my 2-bdrm suite, gave me his phone number, then a couple of minutes later he was gone. Boom! So this is what a Public Adjuster does? That's what mine does.

We ended up staying there for two weeks, enjoying separate beds and baths, with a kitchen and living situation, and free breakfast daily, until the man found suitable temporary digs near my house. I was shocked and relieved when I found out this man's company provided furnishings, rugs, linens, towels, cleaning materials, dishes, utensils, etc.

These provisions were covered by the **Loss of Use** portion of my policy. All we needed was personal toiletries and toothpaste. Well, a rep from the Red Cross contacted me and they provided all that and then some. Family stepped up right away and bought us clothes, shoes, and dinner the night of the fire. Aside from food, and a bath for the white dog covered in soot, which my advance would cover, we were provided everything we could possibly need to keep us for a while.

The day after the fire, I went to the workplace to get my laptop checked out in the IT clinic. The tech opened the device and showed me where black powder and a sticky, tar-like substance had invaded the inside. I was issued a new one, though they said they would try to clean out the existing one. It stands to reason my TVs and other devices also looked like that inside. My PA told me not to plug in any electronics from the house because it could start another fire. I knew he was making sense from what I had seen in that laptop at work. Ew.

Lesson 3: Hire a solid Public Adjuster to help you coordinate all things relating to your loss. My guy represented me with the contractors/vendors, secured my temporary lodging, and walked me through the procedure for my personal property replacement—which should have all been paid for through my insurance claim (more on that later).

When I initially called my insurance company from my front porch, I immediately knew from the tone and the pace that they were going to minimize my advance, my suffering, my inconvenience, my displacement, and everything to do with the fire, because that's just what they do. The companies we pay may cover our loss events, but they are not our representatives—they are agents of the company, and their interest is with the company.

He began his little script, and I hit him with my PA's name and contact information. He tried to put up some resistance, but my guy knows the language and the rules, so he got me a better advance than the zero the agent was trying to give me. The man had cited something like the advance would be a percentage relative to the scope of work to be performed, or something unreasonable like that. Yeah, nah. I got emergency money right away.

And from then on, they dealt with my PA in matters relating to my loss event. I mean, here I was sitting outside in smoky clothes, with not even a toothbrush or a hairbrush, and they wanted to stall me out. Pass.

3

Right time, right place...

The remediation contractor I hired to repair my house was referred to me by someone I knew and trusted. They had worked on something together in the past, and one of their reps was on the site of my fire, so they got the job. I was invited to meet at their office a few weeks after the fire to discuss terms and sign all the documents that would get the project rolling. Finally! Some movement. I was so excited to make changes I'd been dreaming about for years. I had chosen paint colors, designed my new kitchen in my head and on paper, and I could finally ask somebody knowledgeable about taking down some walls.

In the interim, some conversations had occurred about the amount of damage, and an insurance adjuster had done his walk-through. We were just waiting on his report so we could proceed. Apparently, the contractor reps had attended at least one walk-through, because insurance estimates were created, and they came up with their own estimates of what was to be done, and how much it would cost.

Eventually, some agreement was reached, and when I sat down to go over the particulars with the contractor, the numbers were spelled out in terms of what would need to be paid and when. According to the documents, the project would take three months, and I left that meeting flying high.

In the weeks after we got settled in the temporary house, I would visit my house every day to ensure it wasn't broken into or vandalized, and let my son ride his bike, or play with friends. I still took him to his bus stop every morning and afternoon to keep a sense of normalcy. Despite his earlier appearance, the fire had rattled him quite a bit. He was trying to enjoy our hotel stay and our temporary digs, but the thought of another fire was always with him. I assured him this was an isolated incident, but I too was anxious about the whole situation.

At that time, I could let my thoughts flow: *What if my son had been sleeping when the lamp caught fire next to his bed? Or worse, what if he was in his own shower and I didn't hear it? What if we didn't make it down the stairs and got caught in the smoke? What if…?*

The house smelled nasty and had no power, so we didn't spend time inside, but eventually, one day after my son was off to school, I went inside and had a good, ugly cry for what had been lost. Don't get me wrong; I saw the possibilities, and I was thankful to God for covering us, and I was not sad to envision the old replaced with all new. My sadness came from being displaced for a time, and I recalled all the hard work my kids and I had put into that home.

It was only by God's grace that we got the home in the first place. I was at the tail end of my divorce. I had worked on my credit for about 6 months prior to buying it, and a friend of mine had to take me by the hand and show me the process, and the potential in this particular house. I couldn't see anything except failure at the time. Failed marriage. Failed to reconcile. Failed at keeping my credit clean. But I had someone to pull me out of that funk, and I ended up getting this house for a steal. It was a short sale. No way I could've afforded it otherwise.

We moved in when my youngest was a couple of months old. My kids and I touched every surface. We replaced yucky carpet with new flooring. We painted every wall ourselves. We scrubbed and swept and maintained our home—just us. I built things in the garage, I imagined, I taught them life skills and how to turn necessity into something creative and fly. We made this house our home, with our own hands. I had my moment, and then I turned the page to move forward on some much-needed and much-anticipated change. But my excitement would be short-lived.

Lesson 4: The insurance company holds the purse strings. So they send out a certain amount based on the adjuster's approved scope of work to be performed by the contractor. If your property is secured by a mortgage, your mortgage company will be included in the payment chain. You'll have to call them and let them know there's been a loss on the property, provide info from the contractor, and the mortgage company will instruct you what to send them. In my case, there was an online portal for me to upload documents and check the status of each draw (the amount of money released on your behalf).

The cycle is: The insurance company issues payments on the claim for specific things. For this section of your policy, regarding repair of the **Dwelling** and/or **Other Structures**, the funds go to the mortgage company, then the mortgage company sends a draw in increments.

They usually release only a percentage at the beginning, a percentage after about 50% of the work is done, and a final draw near completion. They send their own inspectors to ensure the work has reached these milestones, and then they release funds, with the contractor and you as payees.

If your contractor is not keeping the schedule, the draw will likely not be released on time either. The entities in the process know this is how it works. Most contractors won't start work without that first draw. Well, I didn't know that. I thought once the insurance company released the funds on my behalf, work should have commenced. I mean, the check is in the mail; right? Nah. Ok, so my PA explained all that to me, and it just meant I had to wait a little longer. Fine.

4

About seven weeks into the process...

A few weeks went by, and I expected to see people buzzing around the property, planning, assessing, measuring, a dumpster or something. Nope, crickets. I checked in with my PA and he said there was a holdup because my contractor disagreed with the insurance adjuster; apparently, there were more line items that needed to be added to the scope of work because of local building codes or something. It sounded reasonable....

Late the following month, I was at the property, and I saw one of the contractor reps coming out. She told me they were finally about ready to start work, but they would need to inventory all the items inside the house before they could move it out. I remember asking her why they would move it when most of it was probably trash. I was thinking about my lovely cream-colored leather sofa that was smoky and visibly layered in soot, and my upholstered furniture, and anything obviously damaged by smoke, trampling, or water.

She assured me they needed to catalog each item, pack it, tag it, and remove it from the property so they could finally start putting my house back together. I ran it by my PA, he agreed, as long as they provided me a document with said catalog of items, and I gave the approval.

Maybe a day or two later, I came by the house and there were ladies sitting at the kitchen table counting, marking, packing things. Ok, that's progress. I'm encouraged. During that process, another company came in to gather all the fabrics and wardrobe items from the home to see if they could salvage anything. Clothing, shoes, purses, linens, towels, basically wearable things and textiles.

They said they would send me a list of anything that could not be cleaned/salvaged, and off they went.

When all the other inventory was cataloged, I got an itemized list that was supposed to help me identify what needed to be claimed as a loss when the time came. Anything small or easily carried was removed from the property. Heavy items like furniture was left behind. I thought we were waiting on a dumpster, so we could start rebuilding. Sounded reasonable....

Lesson 5: No items should be removed from the property unless and until the insurance company sends an adjuster to document and identify what can and cannot likely be salvaged. This adjuster will take lots of pictures to document the condition of the items left in the property, and they'll submit their findings to the insurance company for use in determining how much compensation you will receive under the section of your policy dealing with **Personal Property Replacement.**

How this part is handled depends on whether you opted specifically for replacement cost—which costs a little extra in your policy—or if you did not, in which case you'll get the value of the items after depreciation, based on their age. The vast difference is when you have replacement coverage, you'll request the amount those items would cost to replace at today's prices.

To receive this compensation, you'll need to submit an itemized list of everything, sort of like they want you to do when you write off charitable contributions of items. What, how many, when, how much.... Very detailed, very specific. I recommend everyone just go around their homes and snap pics of things to help later on if this process becomes necessary in your life.

5

Fumble! Or was it pass interference?

Not long after I had received my itemized inventory list and reviewed it, I got a call from my PA, telling me we had a problem. Apparently, the adjuster assigned to assess my personal property was not able to do so because my personal property had been removed from the premises prematurely. Surely someone other than me should have foreseen that and timed it better. Why would they pack, wrap or move anything if they knew the adjuster had not yet assessed it?

Remember, they all do this for a living; I, the customer, am out of my depth. But OK, it was decided they would go to the contractor's office and view the items instead. I'm sure that was an arduous task because they had packed and wrapped everything. They just got to undoing all that, and the process continued.

Another month went by with zero activity. I called my PA and asked him what the holdup was. He said they were still waiting on another draw from the mortgage company. That didn't sound reasonable to me, considering it had been two months since we all came to an understanding of what was to be done, how much that should cost, and at least two checks had been received and remitted to them. He told me to call the contractor and ask him what the holdup was.

The response sounded to me like *Blah blah blah, waiting on money; we identified some other things that need to be addressed (3rd time), so the insurance company needs to approve that and release more funds.*

Dude, it's been two months already, and the contract we signed said you'd be done in three. Why are we still at step one, identifying any things???? If they're necessary, why can't we work on those approvals after we at least get started on SOMETHING?

Beyond that, I had reviewed the scope of work myself, and it looked to be pretty spot-on to me. And another thing, why did you have your people lean on me about moving anything out of the house prematurely if you didn't have enough money to start construction? The whole premise was that it was in the way of construction.

At that point, I knew.... I said I need to cancel this contract and move on from this. He said it would cost me 10% of the current SOW on the table. I didn't have that, and I knew the insurance company wouldn't agree to pay that, so I was stuck. To smooth things over, the contractor invited me back to the office later in the week, to pick out finishes and go over the layout and selections for my new kitchen. He said he had been back to the house, taken a look at the walls I wanted to remove, and he was pretty sure he could do it. I wasn't impressed.

When the Project Manager brought in some cabinet samples, I was disgusted and deflated. I distinctly remember saying those looked like something I had in my very first apartment. I'm talking honey oak, half overlay, and looking like they pulled them out of somebody else's 90's reno and had them in the warehouse waiting on a sucker to take them. Clutching my pearls! I think not. I was pissed! It was at that moment that I knew this whole ordeal was definitely going from bad to worse. No doubt in my mind.

I left their office and went directly to my favorite cabinet store, where I designed the kitchen I wanted. They were having a BOGO free promotion, which was right on time for me. I set the date of install for two months out. I had a glimpse of the types of fixtures and other things they were trying to install in my house, so I ordered my own fixtures.

I window shopped at the furniture store, making note of what I wanted and where, basically designing the house I had been dreaming of for several years. I really did miss that sectional though. It was beige leather, with two cushy recliners on one end, a middle wedge, and a queen size pullout bed on the other. That thing was comfortable, and expensive! But after the fire, my perspective changed a bit. I wanted fewer things, and more reasonably priced ones. So I became a resourceful researcher.

The following month, I came by the house one day to see that a port-a-potty had been posted up on my driveway. All kinds of truck drivers would stop and use it daily. I noticed that the electrical panel had been replaced, and new smoke detector lines were being installed. I was cautiously optimistic.

But my temporary housing was scheduled to terminate in that month, because my three months was up. So my PA requested an extension from the insurance company; remember, they were paying my **Loss of Use** expenses. That covered the rental of the temporary home and all the bells and whistles that came with it.

Lesson 6: I had to pay my mortgage, all my usual bills, the cable bill at the temp house, and the utilities on both properties. Although the electric was still shut off at my house, and nobody should've been using the water, I got a water bill that month for hundreds of dollars, like triple my average usage. I hadn't lived there for three months; why?

I was able to pause my cable bill at home until I returned. These types of expenses were partly why I periodically requested advances from the insurance company. It was like being on an expensive vacation, while still taking care of home. And we had to eat. But we had good coverage, so it worked out.

6

Three more months...

So the insurance company approved another month of temporary expenses for us. Work had finally begun. I pushed back my kitchen install twice. And my furniture delivery. In the interim, we had gotten back the report from the adjuster who assessed what was salvageable and what was not. I signed a disposal form with the contractor, authorizing them to destroy whatever they had taken away. I was already working on my inventory list to submit to the insurance company.

By then, I had heard back from the cleaners who took the wearables away, and they sent their bill to the insurance company. Their expenses came out of the **Personal Property Replacement** section of the policy. Once all that was sorted out, I submitted my inventory list to the company so I could replace what was lost in the fire. And then another extension was granted on my temporary digs. They did end up taking out those two walls I wanted gone, though they left a column stuffed with ventilation ducts. I was told it was unavoidable.

The following month, I found out that the contractor never destroyed my personal property. They were still storing it, so my PA told me to ask for it back so we could dispose of it ourselves. Something just didn't feel right. Sure enough, they were still holding on to it. They ended up bringing a lot of it back, but not all of it. I had them load it in the garage, because there was no dumpster, and there was really nowhere else to put it right then.

Oddly enough, I found that my DIY instincts and my years of watching shows about sweat equity, real estate and design were going to be of good use during this ordeal. I started monitoring EVERY-

THING more closely. My PA was doing his part, but I closely scrutinized the SOW to ensure the contractor was doing what they claimed they needed to do.

Would you believe they repeatedly proposed amendments to the SOW, including line items totaling $20,000-$44,000, which were denied by the insurance company repeatedly? Would you believe I informed them that they had not included repairs to areas in my basement with water damage, and they never addressed that in any amendments?

Would you believe they never addressed the broken fence post that occurred when the firefighters gained entry to the back of the house? By now it had been covered by overgrowth of bushes and had the fence leaning and sagging.

I examined every email, request and submission made by the contractor after that. I became the project manager on my own job, though there was one already in place. It's important to note that he worked for the contractor—not me. I asked questions, I pushed back, I used all my skill sets, and I peeped numerous errors, omissions, and discrepancies, which I pointed out every time. I was on site every day. I took so many photos.... I documented everything. My ladder and other things went missing from my garage. I got an alert that my Firestick was being used somewhere other than at my house; purchases were made. So many things went wrong. So many things....

My PA was holding his own with the insurance company, and I was leaning on him pretty hard about the contractor, who was neither doing all the work prescribed in the SOW, nor doing a decent job at what they attempted. I just wanted to go home. But they weren't hearing me, and by then the insurance company wanted us to wrap this thing up because there would be no more lodging extensions. They said the job should not have taken that long to complete. I concur.

In the 6th month after the fire, during my final approved month of temporary lodging, the work just stopped. People stopped showing up, and they stopped responding to our communications. Eventually, I got an invoice and a letter from the contractor accusing me of fraud. It went on to say they would not be returning to my project until the invoice in question was paid in full—a whopping $32,000 in fees.

Apparently, they created and submitted an invoice to my insurance company for payment of packing, moving and storage fees. They were charging me for handling my personal property they insisted they needed to move back in month two, to allow construction to commence.

I didn't expect any such invoice, and we only found out about it because they were charging it against my **Personal Property Replacement** portion of the policy, which had been depleted by then. My cleaners had been paid, my PA had been paid, and I had received the replacement cost of what was declared lost in the fire. They called me a fraud because I received money designated for ME to use in replacing what I lost when MY house caught fire, and THEY didn't have access to that money.

When we saw the invoice in question, it immediately became clear why they had pushed me to get everything out of the house prematurely. It was arranged by date, activity, and the alleged cost for each unit. There were charges for multiple sets of boxes—for the packing, and the unpacking, and the alleged repacking, and the moving vans and the personnel, and an excessive number of days charged for storage of items that were supposed to have been destroyed months prior, and several large dumpsters they never produced. I have photos showing tons of trash in my back yard because there was never any dumpster provided.

The invoice was so contrived, and obviously premeditated. They went so far as to include descriptions of what was allegedly in some of the boxes they allegedly packed. They must've forgotten that they gave me an itemized inventory list 5 months prior, describing what went into each box number, and how many boxes there were in total.

When comparing the box numbers on the new invoice to the old inventory list, they didn't match up. And how did I end up being charged for more boxes the 2nd time they were allegedly packed than I had the 1st time? The devil really is in the details.

Well, there was some discussion between them and the insurance company, and they agreed to pay a portion of the invoice from the **Dwelling** portion of the policy as part of the construction costs, as it was necessary to clear out the property prior to construction. They refused to pay for the storage portion of the invoice. So, the contractor refused to return to my property and complete any work.

I had to relinquish my temporary digs at the end of that month, so I got my new kitchen installed by a contractor working with the cabinet company, I had the electric turned back on, I furnished most of my house, replaced all my kids' items, and moved back home with a soggy, smelly basement and soot stains on the exterior of my home where the smoke had escaped.

The following month, we had a meeting and walkthrough with the contractor's management team, which yielded no results. They sent me two follow-up letters demanding the remainder of the funds from the SOW they never completed, along with the remainder of the bogus invoice charges that were not paid—totaling about $30,000.

It's worth noting that the money from the construction portion was still tied up with the mortgage company, because the work completed had not met the threshold they required in order to release those funds. And the insurance company still held funds they wouldn't release without a signed document from me saying the work was complete.

I had to find another contractor to complete the items from the SOW, including the entire bottom level, paint the exterior trim and soffits, and roughly three months later, the house was completed. All funds were eventually released, and I thought I could move on with my life.

Later, I found out that no permits were ever pulled on the structural work, window retrofitting, interior framing or anything except the heavy up at the electrical panel, which was completed by a different subcontractor. They charged me extra to remove walls that were supporting my upper level, they tucked away much of the electrical wiring from my kitchen; I have no power in my island. And no permit was ever pulled for any of that.

Would you believe the port-a-potty was still on my driveway and no one was servicing it all those months? Yep. My PA and I did some research, sent a couple of Facebook messages, and we had the owners come and remove it. I wish I could say that's the end of the ordeal, but it's not. Would you believe it's still going on today, in 2025? Would you believe it gets even WORSE? Well, hold tight; let me slide this next lesson in here.

Lesson 7: Licensed contractors in the state of Maryland are covered by a guaranty fund, which allows customers to file a claim, go through a process, and potentially get compensation from errors or damages incurred by said licensed contractors. MHIC website has the terms, conditions and timeframes explained for you. Use it if you need it. Would you believe I did not?

I forget how I found out about the fund, but by then, I was pretty much tapped out emotionally. I tried for almost three years to stop being so upset by the thought of those people, their intentions, their actions, and their failure to fulfill our contract. It was so deep, I was embittered, plotting evil against them. How do you just lie, steal and cheat people at their most vulnerable time?

A homeowner's insurance policy holds value for you to lift your property up out of the disastrous state of disrepair it fell into. You paid that policy and kept it in force for times just like this. Don't let anybody steal from you because they think insurance money is up for grabs.

I went to a pretty dark place, so I decided to pray on it and leave it behind me. The house was livable, despite the obvious issues, and some later discoveries of poor workmanship and cut corners. Windows leaking air and water, low quality materials, outlets pulling out of the wall, watery paint that dripped, and on and on. The average person would walk in and not notice anything beyond the amazing design job I did. God, I wish I had filed that guaranty claim. SMH

Lesson 8: My homeowner's policy was up for renewal that summer. It doubled in price. I also learned that information on insurance claims is collected by those 3rd party agencies used by people to find out all about you. They stay on your record for roughly 5 years after the event. So if you were wondering why your rates are ridiculous, one of those companies more than likely provided your claims history. You can request the data directly from those companies and dispute any erroneous info.

*It's off-topic, but my consumer report was ridiculously long and filled with inaccuracies. I quickly cleaned that up. They even had me confused with someone of the same name in another state.

7

Two good things...

Do you know that sometimes God will send you exactly what you need without you having to ask for it? During the ordeal, I learned that my DIY/design hobby was more like a passion. While I was overseeing this and pushing back on that, I felt this incredible sense of purpose. I was drawn to all the things about construction and design, and I wanted to make sure things were being handled properly.

Despite the immediate circumstances, I thoroughly enjoyed the design process, the creative ideas surging through me, and the ease with which I found what I wanted at affordable prices. I partnered with my relief contractor, who later finished my house, and started my renovation company that year. Since starting my own company, I've worked with a number of good, solid tradesmen who have shown me that it's not hard to do a good job if you're skilled and care about your craft.

A few months after starting my renovation & design business, a friend suggested I study for the real estate exam with her. It made sense. I agreed to check it out using a free 5-day trial. I finished the on-line class in two weeks, and was ready for the exam. I got licensed that summer, and I quit my good government job of 30 years.

It really wasn't that good to me, if I'm being honest. I had maxed out on steps, and I was never gonna be a chosen one, sponsored, or recommended to rise anywhere for any reason. My cousin laughs loud and hard at me, and asks me to repeat the story I once told him about how my career stalled out and died in 1993. Wanna hear it? Here it go.

So it was late December, and one of the execs in my division approached me with a request. I thought it was odd, because I didn't work for this man, and I was sure he didn't even know my name. Nevertheless, he asked me to take a subway fare card and go return some books to the Library of Congress on the opposite side of the US Capitol building.

Now, our office was at 500 North Capital Street, just across from Union Station. And the way the subway system was set up, I would need to catch the red line all the way back to Metro Center, just to get a blue or orange line train to Capitol South, and walk to the Library of Congress, then turn around and come back. It was cold out, in December.

The ground was icy. But what gave me pause was the fact that we had two full-time male couriers on staff. Their job was to pick up and deliver all sorts of things, along with some copy room duties. Why, on earth, would that man come and ask me to do that? Then too, the director's secretary had often run errands for the execs that she worked for, and she was provided with a taxi voucher each time. All things considered, I politely declined.

Well, that didn't go over too well. The white-haired man's face turned beet red, and he turned and left in a huff. I was not at all bothered, because I was sure I had done the right thing. The next day, my supervisor came back into the office, and he just shook his head as he passed my desk, but not in a shameful way; it was more like cursing my name, because he had just gotten chewed out or something.

I did feel bad for him, but what were these people trying to prove by asking me to go out and freeze my feet off while doing somebody else's job? And that's the day my career at IRS died. I wasn't fired, but I was nobody's favorite. My only regret, though, is having stayed as long as I did after I knew it would not serve me.

But anyway, I did my 30 years, and I walked away with a new plan that I was beyond excited about. You couldn't tell me nothing. I already had a baking business going on the side when I started this company. My little business was booked and busy. My first year in real estate and design, I brought in revenues double my salary at IRS. The following year, I almost tripled my former salary. Third year, I didn't top that, but I still brought in significantly more than my former salary.

You know what was even better than that? I was happy. I loved my new job. I felt like I was born for this. To this day, it's the only kind of work I want to do. And had the fire not forced me into that arena, I might not have pursued it fully. I had only dabbled in design prior to that. Helped people with styling and selection for free. For fun. It's a lot more fun getting paid handsomely for work that you also love.

I got some bad news in that third year, though. Just before the three-year mark after that contractor ordeal, I was served with a court summons from them claiming some $50,000+ for breach of contract. I called my PA friend and told him. We were both stuck on stupid that day.

He did a lot of cussing, and some apologizing. Then I called up a couple of attorneys I had worked with before and scheduled consultations. The first attorney said he didn't have time to dedicate to a lawsuit like that because of other obligations. I met with the other attorney, we agreed on his retainer, and we got to work.

But I was sick and quite pissed knowing I could've filed that guaranty claim. I didn't even know all the things that had gone wrong at that point, but I had enough to start with. It was going to be a lengthy process that required me to hire and pay professionals willing to testify and refute what that contractor had said and done, which was a tall order. But it certainly would've given me more credibility and perhaps leverage.

Lesson 9: Part of adulting nowadays includes having some lawyer money. I swear, it seems like as soon as you get anything of value, somebody is trying to take it from you. Yep, buy one of those monthly legal plans, or cuff you some stacks of lawyer money. It could be an auto accident, a contractor, your kid in trouble, your business being sued, or any unexpected thing that puts your peace and personal assets at risk. Unfortunately for me, I have only one asset to pull from—my home. Now that's coming back to bite me....

8

Discovery and depositions…

Discovery and depositions…

Your girl had receipts for days! I prepared my package for my attorney so well, I think he was overwhelmed with the amount of documentation I provided. First, I created a timeline of events. I provided emails. I picked apart their amendments to show they were double dipping on some of the charges. I had photos with timestamps. I had text chains. I had every document I ever signed.

Part of their claim was that they did complete the work. I had letters from them, on their letterhead, explicitly saying they would not come back and finish my job. Part of their itemization of the amount allegedly owed was from one of the amendments that was denied, and therefore never performed. I had the email chain to prove it. It was so obvious….

We exchanged interrogatories with the plaintiff. They declined to answer most of mine, claiming the questions were too vague. Now does that even sound like me? C'mon! I laid out my defense in a way that anyone unfamiliar with construction could follow it. I organized it according to the exhibits submitted with their complaint. I made a notation on each document identifying which interrogatory and exhibit it corresponded to. A blind man could see that my evidence directly contradicted their claims.

It occurred to me that maybe they thought people don't keep good records, so it would work. I thought maybe they had done this before, and it did work. Or maybe people don't even get this far, and they simply settle. I started doing some research to see what I could find out. After I had presented my case and my research, my attorney asked me to settle. I wish you could see the look on my face, then and now. Was he even paying attention?!

In my mind, settling was like admitting fault or wrongdoing. Hard pass. I did everything I was supposed to do. I am the injured party here. So we continued on the path. Shortly before they were scheduled to depose me, I got a call from my attorney telling me he would be unable to continue at that time because he was being temporarily suspended from the bar. Work. Of. The. Devil! He sent out a formal letter, and both sides agreed to put things on pause while I retained new counsel, or until he came back—whichever happened first. Only I couldn't afford to hire a SECOND attorney.

Eventually, my time expired, and so did my efforts to retain new counsel. I just couldn't do it. Everyone I spoke to wanted many thousands of dollars for this kind of case. I couldn't understand why this case made so many lawyers act funny. I thought: *I did all the hard work for you!* Some things I will never understand. It is what it is, though.

Would you believe that at the end of everything, I was without an attorney, and I lost? Yep. I was ultimately sanctioned for not sitting for their deposition, all my evidence was moot, and they won a judgment against me.

9

The $100,000 Bill...

The $100,000 Bill...

All in all, with their $50,000 claim, plus interest, penalties, and attorney's fees, I now owe these people over $100K. I appealed, but it was denied. I was sick for a while. Physically, emotionally, mentally unable to move through my life the way I used to.

I tried to cling to my faith and look for the lesson, but I have no idea what the lesson is this time. Still. If you have any ideas, please share them with me. I'm struggling. That's partly why I'm writing this book; I just need to release this anger, this rage. I was completely taken advantage of. But it just keeps on coming.

After they won the judgment, they immediately began hunting around for my bank accounts, garnishing. You wanna know something though? People think I have money for some reason. Like I'm stashing coins here and there. My only tangible asset is this house. I've built quite a bit of equity in it over the years—for my family. If there is a lesson, I would say use your equity to acquire additional assets. Don't let it sit there. It could become a noose around your neck later.

The trick to my lifestyle is I live simply, take care of my family and our home, I rely on God for direction and to supply me with whatever I need. I don't bother anybody, and I put my creative talents to use every chance I get. I don't buy things I don't need, aside from an occasional treat or a paint job somewhere in my house.

I might buy a pink chair or a colorful rug I've been stalking online, but only when it's a steal. I hate overspending on things when I know I can find a better deal. That's why I'm so good at my job too. I respect my clients' budgets, and their efforts to enjoy nice things in their personal space. There's no gold mine here; just my mind.

As for the noose around my neck, there wasn't any secret stash to attack, so they used their judgment to come for my house. I ended up filing bankruptcy to avoid that. However, because of the equity in my property, I can only file Chapter 13, and I have to pay out to my creditors, now including them, the amount of equity I have in the property. Or I can file Chapter 7, let the court take my house and sell it to pay off my creditors. That's the picture today.

Could I begin again? I honestly doubt it. I have nothing left in me at this time. I simply do not have the bandwidth. What am I gonna do? Pray and keep it moving. I'm at the mercy of a different court now, and I always say there's an appeal in heaven. We shall see how it goes. It is what it is.

I know some of you are thinking I missed a very important lesson, which is with God in my corner, I should be more optimistic, more faithful, more something; right? You have a point there. But I thought it was important to be truthful, honest, forthcoming about how I sometimes feel as a result of this years-long ordeal.

We often wanna jump right to the sunny side of the street and tell people to straighten up because everything will be OK. And I'm not disagreeing with you on that. I know it will. I consistently go to the Lord and ask for just a measure of strength to get through my trials. And I carry on, reminding myself, *I'm building endurance. His thoughts are higher than my thoughts. He will not abandon me.* If worse comes to worst, maybe he'll give me a new house like he gave me this one.

The reality is some days we need to pick ourselves up off the floor and drag ourselves through the day, or the next hour or whatever. And that's just life. I acknowledge all my feelings and flaws. I respect the grief process. It comes in waves, regardless of what was lost. I'm grieving the loss of my former lifestyle, my freedom and flexibility as a hard-working adult, my credit profile, my largest savings account. I'm grieving a lack of good options.

I have to work the next 5 years to pay somebody who's essentially stealing from me. Let that sink in. The irony is if they had just done a good job, I would've sent quality referrals. I can't help but wonder if maybe they aren't capable of doing a good job. I watched a lot of the work as it was being done; it didn't appear to me that these were skilled tradespeople. I did like the painter's technical skill; he stood out, even though the paint they chose was one I would never use.

What if part of the business plan has become to use cheap labor, cheap products, and put customers in a position to owe you above and beyond the policy payouts, so you can end up suing them? If you get the judgment and they pay the base amount, plus interest, and your attorney's fees, what have you really lost by retaining counsel for the suit?

What if part of the strategy now is to amend the SOW as often as possible and get the insurance companies to pay out more on each claim without you having to actually buy materials and do that work? How would they even know? How many times, how often do you think a company could do that without getting caught? How much revenue do you think a company could generate doing things that way for decades? Sounds kinda ridiculous when I think about it. Who would actually do that? That's crazy; no one would do that. Right?

We never did find out why that lamp spontaneously combusted that day. But because of that event, I got to review my career options, updated the interior style of my home, remodeled my kitchen, bought the good appliance package with the double oven & door-in-door fridge that lights up when you knock on it. I got to prove to myself and others that my professional value extends beyond that dead-end role I inhabited at IRS.

I now create design plans that enhance people's lives and align with my passion and purpose. I oversee their construction projects, procure materials and advocate for the clients to prevent waste, fraud and abuse of their hard-earned money. I treat my clients with decency, respect, and genuine concern for their well-being. I don't know if you understand how much joy I have because of these things. I have purpose. I have value. I have power.

Maybe I had to go through this so I could help somebody else avoid it. Maybe some practices and people need to be exposed, and just maybe I can help with that. That's my prayer anyway. Have you experienced anything like this? Please share your experience. If I can help you with anything, kindly reach out through one of my social media channels, or the Contact page on my website. Be well. Live fully. Onward.

Tonya D Floyd
Author, Real Estate Professional, Lifestyle Consultant
FB: Signature Lifestyle Solutions
IG: makesignaturemoves
TikTok: signaturemovestdf
YouTube: @tonyadfloyd
https://makesignaturemoves.com

Tonya D Floyd is a published Author, Real Estate Professional and Lifestyle Consultant from Washington, DC. Her published works date back to 2005, and include fiction, nonfiction, poetry and self-awareness titles with a focus on relationships and family life. Tonya pursued adult studies in Psychology, Communication and Business at the University of MD (currently Global Campus). She is also a retired federal government employee.

Some of Tonya's favorite things are dessert, design and decor. Her love for creating beautiful and flavorful things gave birth to her company, Signature Lifestyle Solutions, which offers custom solutions and targeted recommendations to make home/lifestyle/business more manageable for its clients. Specialties include real estate, renovation, design, culinary, planning/logistics, and some personal care services.

Tonya has also written editorials on various topics for the Prince George's Post newspaper, and was a contributor to the blog *Colors of Women* in 2009 and 2010. She manages her own blog, *From the Mind of Tonya D Floyd*, and offers her perspective on various topics through her *Epiphany* podcast. You can learn more about Tonya and her work through her website at: makesignaturemoves.com

www.ingramcontent.com/pod-product-compliance
Lightning Source LLC
LaVergne TN
LVHW060045210926
848481LV00013B/3961
9798869121134